Confessions of a Barefaced Woman

Confessions of a Barefaced Woman

poems

Allison Joseph

Red Hen Press | *Pasadena, CA*

Book layout by Madison R. Foster

Library of Congress Cataloging-in-Publication Data
Names: Joseph, Allison, 1967–author.
Title: Confessions of a barefaced woman / Allison Joseph.
Description: First edition. | Pasadena, CA: Red Hen Press, [2018]
Identifiers: LCCN 2017029207 | ISBN 9781597096096 (softcover: acid-free paper) |
    ISBN 9781597097550
Subjects: LCSH: African American women—Poetry.
Classification: LCC PS3560.O7723 A6 2018 | DDC 811/.54—dc23
LC record available at https://lccn.loc.gov/2017029207

The National Endowment for the Arts, the Los Angeles County Arts Commission, the Ahmanson Foundation, the Dwight Stuart Youth Fund, the Max Factor Family Foundation, the Pasadena Tournament of Roses Foundation, the Pasadena Arts & Culture Commission and the City of Pasadena Cultural Affairs Division, the City of Los Angeles Department of Cultural Affairs, the Audrey & Sydney Irmas Charitable Foundation, the Kinder Morgan Foundation, the Meta & George Rosenberg Foundation, the Allergan Foundation, the Riordan Foundation, and the Amazon Literary Partnership partially support Red Hen Press.

First Edition
Published by Red Hen Press
www.redhen.org

ACKNOWLEDGMENTS

Poems from this collection previously appeared in *Atlanta Review, Baltimore Review, Chiron Review, Connecticut Review, El Dorado Poetry Review, Folio, Green Mountains Review, Lake Effect, Limestone Circle, Pacific Coast Journal, Perceptions, Quercus Review, Soundings East, Shenandoah, Sidewalks, Smartish Pace, Spillway, Spindrift, Spoon River Poetry Review, Sundog: the Southeast Review, Tamaqua, Tongue: A Literary and Visual Arts Journal, Verseweavers,* and *Wellspring.*

Contents

ON THE SUBWAY

It was comic on *Seinfeld*: Jerry looks up to see a naked man
across the aisle, an unfolded *New York Times* placed
strategically over his lower girth. They trade insults
and fat jokes, banter like Abbott and Costello by episode's end.
But it isn't funny on the number six train
when I look up from my chem book, see a man
across the aisle both clothed and exposed,
his pants held up by rope, dirt clumped in his matted hair,
long body sprawled out, limbs splayed, head wobbling.
He wears a tattered jacket, sleeves too short for his arms,
no shirt beneath, fly open, revealing bare skin, a limp penis.
He nods and wakes, rocking to the subway car's motion,
and I fear if I rise, go one car over, I will rouse him,
and he will follow. No one here but us, no other passengers
clutch metal poles or lean against the walls as the train
hurtles further into the Bronx. They've long since
noticed his smell, this man whose shoes flap loose,
his brown skin deadly grey, eyes bloodshot and raw.
I'm silent as he sways, tugs on the rope around his waist,
turning my head away from the thought
of what he might move, how he might reach across
this chugging car. I don't stir, put my textbook
in front of my face, hope that because he's black
and I'm black that he won't hurt me.
I am one stop from my stop, but when the train
reaches Parkchester, I dart through the closing doors,
knowing I'm too far from home to walk.

In the Public Library

In silence, in shadow, this girl reads words—
sounds discrete as bricks, jagged as shards

of bottles smashed against the library's
concrete steps, its entrance an alley

reeking of piss, booze, its pavement
giving way, cracked along city fault lines.

Inside, one room of warmth and dirt,
floor wax and gum wrappers, paperbacks

thumbed and stamped with inky due dates,
hardcovers wrapped in yellowed cellophane,

tables and chairs with initials carved
into them, damage sunk deep in wood.

Here I learn the potency of words,
their sounds resounding in my head,

ears, equilibrium shaken,
words destined for my preteen ribcage,

my body a bony geometry. Here,
the hours teem with voices, their rhythms;

coiled tense, I lean on words and love
all this—broken bindings, smudged print,

fondled pages, my library card,
warm slip frayed in my taut grip.

FUTURE DOCTOR

Pretending for Mother's sake to be interested in medicine,
I'd go to school Saturdays too, ride the train
from the Bronx to Manhattan's high-rise hospitals
for special classes for gifted students, bright minority kids,
future doctors. What I remember most aren't equations

or experiments, brilliant liquids poured from one test tube
to another, into beakers, or the friendly med students
who tried to make a scientist of me, despite stolid resistance.
What I remember most are the bodies, cadavers laid out
on metal slabs, skin cold, clammy after formaldehyde.

During the week, medical students sawed and flayed
these anonymous people, not knowing on weekends
high school students studied their cuts: chest cavities
pried open, ribcages splayed. I was never much good
at telling one organ from another, fascinated instead

by the waxy, sticky buildup of cholesterol in bloodless
arteries. I didn't quite know what we were looking for—
their legs rigid, skin over them mottled, yellowish-
brown and gray, unsettling sepia—wasn't sure
how dead bodies could make my future better,

only knowing my mother wanted a doctor
in our family, her own lungs cancer-heavy,
her dream to live to see me graduate. Dutiful,
I'd spend Saturdays examining empty hands,
stiffened fingers, limbs and torsos,

tendons and ligaments stringy, stretched,
muscles drained yet fibrous. I tried
not to stare at faces, at gaping nose holes,
slack but rubbery ears, at mouths
I could push open, then push shut.

BAD DOGS

Neighbors trained their dogs mean,
fenced them and chained them,
whipped their flanks with rope
or wire, until their dogs would pounce
on any stranger happening by.
Didn't matter whether the dog
was terrier or Pekingese, boxer
or mongrel, neighborhood dogs
could yelp themselves into such fury
that there were houses I'd hurry past
coming home from school, book bag
bouncing on my shoulder, socks
sagging around skinny ankles.
So when one sudden fist of a dog
leapt up to bite me, his teeth
piercing two red rows below the crook
of my arm, I scurried home even faster
to show my father the damage.
He went to start a shouting match
with the dog's owner, both of them
yelling, cursing, the dog's owner
in Spanglish, my father in threats
of wrathful retribution.

Fearing rabies, Father pulled me
by my other arm, sat me in the car,
and drove me to Jacobi Hospital,
where I waited on a hard-backed chair,
clutching my arm, peering at the punctures
that scrap of a dog had made,

while gunshot victims rolled past
on metal gurneys. When a young doctor
finally approached, he chuckled,
said *I think you'll live*, then shot me
with some syringe that made my arm
ache more. He turned away, laughing,
white back soon lost as I watched him
return to the business of consoling
the mothers of the newly dead.

First School Dance

You sway to the music
but stick to the wall,
too shy and self-conscious,
alone in the hall.

You're no smiling beauty,
your brown hair's uncurled.
You're thin and flat-chested—
an awkward young girl.

The couples walk past you
as if you're not there.
A freshman in high school,
you think they don't care

about what you're feeling,
about what you see.
Will anyone listen?
You're no prodigy.

I know what it feels like
to stand there all night.
I wish I could tell you
that you'll be all right.

But I have no solace
for what life might hold,
won't offer the knowledge
I know you've been told—

that your life will get better,
your skin will grow clear,
your shape will develop,
you'll lose all the fears

that keep you from dancing
except in your room.
For now, keep your spine straight,
don't slouch into gloom,

remember these moments
won't matter so much
when you've learned your body
is worthy of touch.

FATHER'S MOTHER

How miserable you were,
unable or unwilling to do
comforting things expected
of grandmothers: making
pies or bedtime stories,
gardening on arthritic knees.
You had no friends that I
could see, attended no church,
loved no one but my father,
showed that love by whining
that you wanted to go back
to Grenada, only American insulin
keeping you in the States,
the diabetes he inherited
your only link. I never
saw you hug or kiss,
and you gave him a name
he could never live up to—
Everest—pinnacle of mountains,
highest of destinies. Did you
not touch my father because
his father left you, even though
you were the lightest-skinned
woman in the village?
Did you not touch my father
because his father had other
women, other sons? It's hard
to picture you smiling—
in family photos your face
is stern, lips pressed together,

cat eye glasses hard around
suspicious eyes, tight curls
swept from your forehead.
I was too dark for you to love,
you who were proud to call yourself
"Grenada white." So all
I carry of yours is a name—
Elaine—your first, my middle—
name of burden, of complaint.

READING ROOM

Back before we all became "multicultural,"
when blacks were beautiful in dashikis
and righteous rage, my father sold books
in Toronto, books of pride, sorrow, anger,

an inventory that ended up
in our living room in the Bronx,
a reading room I'd sneak into
when I wasn't supposed to,

my chore and duty there to dust
the coffee tables and knickknacks—
souvenir ashtrays from Caribbean isles,
ebony elephants and pelicans,

hand-carved, foreign-wrought.
Mixed in among my mother's
nursing texts, her medical dictionary
and anatomical tomes, I found

Frantz Fanon's *Black Skin, White Masks*,
a book too severe for my preteen brain,
polysyllabic paragraphs sailing past
my short-sighted mind, Cleaver's

Soul On Ice, which I read fervently,
loving every curse, every mention of sex,
missing the revolution in his prose
in pursuit of dirty words, staring

at the cover, captivated by Eldridge's
prison-saddened face. *Up From Slavery,*
Manchild in the Promised Land,
The Crisis of the Negro Intellectual,

poems of Cèsaire and Senghor—those books
filled me with legacy, history, located me
with Jesse Owens, blazing his body
past fascism as he triumphed

at Hitler's Olympics, with Jackie Robinson
through minor and major league hatreds,
with George Washington Carver as he
synthesized genius from peanuts.

Malcolm X spoke to me from the cover
of his autobiography, black-and-white
photo faded, but his face still sharply
turned upward, his finger up, out,

to signal the better world beyond us.
Could I join these men if I let words
dream in me, if I struggled, didn't
settle, my gaze as bold and forthright

as Frederick Douglass's, Booker T.'s?
Wiping each book clean, I kept that room's
order, my torn rag mottled, spotted,
dark with that week's dust.

Childhood Ballade

Where have they gone, those girls who ran
the dusty urban streets I knew?
We came in every shade: blue-black to tan,
alert to find some mischief to pursue.
We'd run our one-block avenue,
ashy legs caught up in speedy games,
frantic to chase a ball somebody threw.
Where are those girls who used to sing my name?

We'd duck behind a car or garbage can,
tripping on the laces of our shoes,
knees crashing into asphalt, the span
from thigh to knee bruised and blue
from falls and skids. We'd unscrew
the caps of hydrants, hair untamed
as we danced in spray, broke that taboo.
Where are those girls who used to chant my name?

We'd dig through mud, despite the ban
our mothers yelled at us, the slew
of illnesses we'd get from dirty hands.
Our dirty scabs and scars accrued
but still we picked at skin, planned
more exploits where we'd blame
all damage on bigger kids, their crew.
Where are those girls who used to shout my name?

Back then, who cared about a man,
what one could do for us, what claims
a man might make? I miss them, my noisy fans.
Where are those girls who used to know my name?

GROWN-UP SHOES

How could I forget
your cruel, inflexible soles,
chunky, stacked heels
pitching me forward to wobble
like those Fisher-Price dolls
that didn't fall down,
ankle straps burning
into tender skin, leaving
red welts that softened to scars
days later? The heel cups
flayed skin, left blisters,
forced me to walk funny,
to limp and weep at my first
boy-girl party, a sixth-grade
graduation celebration.
How eagerly I'd awaited
your coming, pleased
when Mother let me choose you
from a mail order catalog's
pages, how stylish you looked
there—beige to match
my party dress, 2 ½ inches high
to make me tall, slim,
give me legs and calves
to make the other girls go home.
But what looked beige
on the page looked yellowed
on my feet, what looked sexy
in photos made my legs
into stalks, feet into boats.

So I didn't dance with that boy
who'd been hitting me all year,
or walk to the table loaded
with cake, chips, punch.
I sat, hard plastic chair
under my flat rear,
flower in my hair losing
each petal, toes jammed together,
barely peeking from the hole
at the tip of each sorry shoe.

Perfect Ride

It may have been a hand-me-down,
a dull olive green, but I wanted
my sister's bike more than
anything, impatient to grow
past my baby bike, its training

wheels, childish fringe.
I wanted to ride in the street,
not on the sidewalk, to know
the feel of bumpy tires over
uneven asphalt, rearing back

so the front wheel rose
into the air, magnificent.
I wanted the speed the older kids
took for granted, rush of furious
pedaling, no hands on handlebars.

Maybe I'd juice it up, paint
it red with racing stripes,
wrap my radio to one handlebar
with a bunch of rubber bands.
Maybe I'd race the boys

on this old three-speed,
winning though their bikes
were bigger, tougher—motocross models,
savage ten-speeds. So when I rode,
I rode, whipping around corners,

dodging cars and double dutch games,
jeering at little girls who still
drew hopscotch grids on safe sidewalks.
No wonder they didn't help me
when I hit a rock and tumbled

forward, laughing louder as I
picked glass from palms, elbows,
my knees small messes of blood.
Weeks later, when I was ready
to ride again, to pedal

where the big kids pedaled,
I found the front tire flat, limp,
so I gave up, kicked it to a corner,
didn't pester my father to patch
then pump the leaky tire.

Sulky child, I no longer cared,
my ride no longer perfect or intact,
boasts no longer effortless.
That bike grew rust in the garage,
no one to stir its spokes.

Spirit of '76

That summer we abandoned little girl pursuits
to gawk up at our television screens
at adorable Nadia, so agile as she posted

perfect ten after perfect ten, and more
adorable still as she stammered in fractured
English, gold medals so heavy around her neck

she seemed weighted to the ground.
She made it look so effortless that we
became convinced we could be gymnasts too,

turned our parents' beds into trampolines,
transformed the arms of worn recliners
into vaulting horses, tried to make

a banister substitute for uneven parallel
bars. Once I turned a cartwheel
on the day the dining room set

was being hauled off, spun then struck my foot
on the chandelier, almost ripping it free
from its socket in the ceiling.

I thought I'd be in trouble, exiled
to my room after a spanking that'd
make my rear hurt far more than my foot.

But my father laughed out loud
when I claimed Nadia made me do it.
Now Nadia is no longer an athlete,

but more of a celebrity, hawking fitness
shoes and tapes, knowing the little girls
who wanted to be like her now have

little girls of their own, or at least
have thighs that say they might.
She tours still, does shows from arena

to arena, but it seems so odd to pay
to witness the gymnastics equivalent
of a rock-n-roll oldies show.

It doesn't seem fair at all
that we're all older now,
no longer breaking the rules

then blaming it on some Romanian girl
with a toothy grin, ponytail,
and her own theme song.

LITTLE BROTHERS

Little brothers stink, I say to Charmaine,
whose little brothers, Ronnie and John,
are filthy creatures happiest when kicking
and karate-chopping through life, confident

in the power of the foot to right wrongs,
settle disputes, especially ones with girls
whose idea of fun is dolls: boy dolls and girl
dolls dressed in precious doll clothes,

eating little doll meals from little doll
plates. Little brothers say yuck to dolls
unless one of them is G.I. Joe, who'll
blow all the rest to plastic bits with

his hand grenade. Little brothers love
superheroes, especially Ronnie, who,
dressed in his pajamas with a towel
tied around his neck, leapt from the

second-story window to the backyard,
hollering, *Look at me, I'm Superman!*
while Charmaine was supposed to be
watching him. He didn't get hurt

pretending to fly, and Mr. Hunt didn't
just pretend to whip Ronnie's behind
when he came home from work.
Little brothers hate to bathe, but love

to hurl water balloons down
to pavement below, aiming for
groups of screeching girls playing jacks.
Little brothers break things, especially

John, who pranced around the living room
in his underwear to play gun-toting bandit,
pulling down ashtrays and lamps,
a stocking over his face for a mask.

I don't have little brothers, and I'm
glad, 'cause Charmaine has to cook
and clean up after them, blamed when
something gets broken, 'cause she's

oldest, the only girl, she should
know better. I don't have any brothers at all,
so when I go home there's silence, no beastly
boys to yell at, squeal on, get even with.

ADVICE ON BEING A PESKY LITTLE SISTER

Sit on your sister's records,
especially if she's saved for them
for weeks, shattering favorites first—
Stevie Wonder and the Spinners,
unplayable on the living room's
hi-fi console. You've already
broken the stereo in her room,
claiming you tripped on loose wires.
Ransack her closet when she's not
around: find lip gloss and eyeshadow
to wiggle fingers in, try on her shoes
then tangle them to a mess of buckles,
snaps, laces. Filch and crease
her magazines, ones she buys,
hoards away—*Cosmo* and *Glamour*
full of photos of skinny women
wearing clothes that cost more
than a year's worth of phone bills.
Oh, about the phone: if her friends call,
tell her they didn't, or tell her they called
to say they left without her and won't
be by to pick her up. If a boy should call,
yell his name as loud as you can,
so your parents are sure to know
who this week's crush is. If a boy
should dare to visit, bring your best friend
for back-up, ruin his attempts
to get closer on the couch by chattering
nonstop, drawing loopy pictures
of them both, flattering portraits

you claim are suitable for framing.
Drive him from your house screaming
all the way home to Jersey,
then beg your sister to know
when he's coming back.

PENMANSHIP

I wrote too slowly, teachers groaned,
laboring over letters and words as if
each one crafted was meant to be
a work of art. I couldn't help it,
I loved the cursive loops—the L,
the H, the strings of S slithering
across ruled paper. When I got older,
teachers swore, *Write faster,*
get all I say down, until I no longer
cared what I was writing, but wrote
for the physicality of it, spreading
ink over paper until my hands
were blue with it. Then one teacher
put a long, skinny, plastic quill
in my hands, showed me how
to hold it at 90 degrees, to dip
the metal nib into ink so dark
it seeped for good into the wood
of the art room's shaky tables.
She chided us to take this writing
slow, to hold this pen like no other,
our touch delicate to free the ink,
but firm to make the letters look
like they'd sprung up from the pages
of a medieval scribe. Finally, she said,
Be proud of the ink your hands collect,
of letters you've shaped without speaking.

NOTHING BUT WORDS

could comfort me, so I sat in the armchair
silently, hoping somehow my presence
could make your bed rest easier,

your lungs no longer home to ache and cough.
You smiled to see your youngest, lanky at 15,
secretive, that girl, with her words and pages

—asked, *What are you writing, what are you writing?*
with breath that faltered from your failing lungs,
past your lips, lips too dry, cracked. Too weak

to lift your arms, you needed help to grasp
the plastic water tumbler always at bedside.
Ashamed, I knew my poems were too dainty

for that sickroom, precious but hardly powerful
enough, not nearly as stately as the daily prayers
you craved, piped in on gospel radio.

I should have showed you what about words
engaged me so, should have read
my shaky scrawl aloud—nothing good

about my shyness, my silence,
nothing shared except your hushed query,
a question I would not answer.

My Tutor

His was the first pocket protector
I'd ever seen. He wore short sleeves
in winter, cardigans Mr. Rogers might
reject, shoes like an orderly's.
But how old was he? What did he do
for fun? Did he have a wife, or lover,
or son or daughter? Or did he spend
all his days peering over those spectacles,
patiently explaining equations to the
mathematically challenged, head tilted
as if too heavy for his neck?
Everyone knew him in that tenement
neighborhood off Fordham Road,
you could ask any kid for Mr. Ottinger—
the man whose students came to him,
a man who came and went so silently
no one questioned what business
a white man had being there.
But did he actually live there?
Sleep and dream there?
Was he a grad school refugee,
too timid to survive, too brilliant
to stray from math? No matter.
He could make all those terrible theorems
make sense, proofs like music under
his tutelage, gestures to be remembered,
not just used then forgotten by semester's
end. He made me feel as if I were smart,
like he was sharing his shortcuts
with only me, head nodding at the end

of his neck, nose sharp, face narrow,
angled like the angles he taught me
secrets of. No one else could make
a pencil dance that fast—not my teachers,
whose tests made me cry, not my mother,
whose faith in Ottinger was so great
she paid him weekly in hopes he could fix
my faulty brain, make me whip-smart, college-bound.
And for the half-hours in his apartment, I was,
our heads close together, necks strained
over a textbook's tiny diagrams,
light from one lamp barely filtering
over the pages, as if neither of us
really needed to see.

For Beauty's Sake

When my mother catches me scraping my legs
with a sixty-nine cent razor and the lather
from the plastic soap dish's dead-end slivers,
she's astonished. This is one beauty tip
she's never heard, and she's perplexed
by my need to pare the hair off my legs.
Why do that to yourself, your legs
just need lotion, she says, staring
at me like she doesn't know whose daughter
this is, her brow furrowed, lips pursed.
I want to explain, tell her my magazines
have decreed hairy legs to be the worst
things a teenage girl can possess, worse,
even, than bad breath. I shrug my shoulders,
claim that everyone says my legs look
better this way. *Who, in God's name,*
is everyone? she counters, arms folded
across her chest, starting in on me with,
If everyone jumped off a bridge, would you too?—
just like I knew she would, just like
she has for fourteen years. Mute, I
mope at my reflection, mope over
my prickly face sore with zits,
my hair that just won't grow,
Afro Sheen or no Afro Sheen.
A laugh bubbles up out of my mother—
Who's gonna feel your legs but you?
Don't come crying to me when you
cut yourself! She leaves me there,
my right hand trembling in its slick

grip on the razor, right leg propped
on the bathtub's slippery rim.
When the first red line surfaces
on my brown knee, I know better
than to ask where the Band-Aids are.

DINNER HOUR

My sister and I would bring books
to the dinner table, trying to avoid
speaking to my father, but angering him
even more, making him curse us,

our books, our rudeness. We were
good-for-nothing, lazy, clumsy,
and stupid, always stupid,
which sounded more like *shtupid*

in his fierce accent. Between bites
of my mother's stewed chicken,
her rice and peas cooked in
coconut milk, he told us what a

waste we were, how we never
turned off lights when we left
a room, and did we think he
was made of money? What

was he to do with us—older one
mouthing off in ignorance,
younger following everything
her sister said, did? Mother,

silent in the narrow kitchen,
rumbled pots in the sink,
cast iron pot on the stove
heavy, greasy with cooking.

We'd put our books down
to eat our dinner—we'd
tried to be good and failed,
made him a man with

children who didn't listen,
daughters who broke dishes,
dropped glasses on the carpet,
splashing its green with accidents

that would not scrub out.
Only when Mother says,
Joe, eat your food,
does reprieve come, her way

of saying, *That's enough.* But we can't
do enough to please a father who can't
be pleased, who points out the damage
we inflict on his floors, his house.

First Concert

For months, Charmaine and I worshipped them,
chirping along to their bubblegum disco singles,
savoring every word written in *Right On!* magazine
about Olympia, Leon, Charmaine, James,
Edmund, Ricky, Angie, Pat and Foster,
—the Sylvers—a discount version of the Jacksons
who topped the charts for a week in 1976
with "Boogie Fever," thrilling eight-year-olds like us,
giving rise to serious debate over who was cuter—
Foster, the youngest, or Edmund, who sang lead
on that immortal track. Charmaine loved the group
because she shared a name with a member,
begged her momma to take us to see them,
until she relented and we rode the subway
down to the Felt Forum to see the Sylvers
live on stage, so excited we could hardly
sit in our seats, bouncing up and down
as the stage lights swirled around us.
But it grew later and later with no Sylvers
in sight, the show held up because
the opening act hadn't yet arrived,
and when it did, we couldn't have been
more disappointed—five men wearing
blue polyester suits with ruffles, blue hats
with turned-up brims, Blue Magic singing
"Sideshow," a song that had been a big hit
two summers before, an eternity ago
as far as we were concerned. We wanted
to boo them off the stage, not knowing
this group was the epitome of Philly soul,

not caring for the lead singer's tearful falsetto.
We wanted Foster's falsetto, not men
trying to sound like boys, so we sat
stonily through their set, applauding
when they left, cheering when the Sylvers
burst on stage, all nine of them dramatic
in metallic skin-tight outfits that made them
look like aliens from an all-black planet.
We screamed our little-girl voices hoarse
for a group no one remembers today, wanting
to be part of that family—adored, adorable,
their voices echoing from every radio on the block.

ADOLESCENT CONFESSION

When I was a girl,
I had such bony legs—
a flat body, no breasts.
To compensate, to cheat—
I stuffed my bra, hoping to be hot.
What a pathetic sight.

I had terrible eyesight,
known as the coke-bottle girl.
I looked anything but hot—
shaky, stick figure legs,
a propensity to cheat,
coward with tissue paper breasts.

I knew that big breasts
could give a girl special insights,
eliminating any reasons to cheat.
I wanted to be the girl
with major cleavage, endless legs,
a body every boy would call hot.

What was it like to be hot?
To feel a boy's hands on your breast,
his fingers between your legs?
Boys, I knew, avoided me on sight—
I wasn't the right kind of girl.
Rumor had it on tests I'd cheat.

I knew it was wrong to cheat,
but, hey, I'd never be hot,

and cheating's all that's left to a girl
lacking curves and breasts,
cursed with blurred sight,
the school's skinniest legs.

Years later, I like my legs,
can't recall when last I cheated.
Chic glasses fix my sight;
I feel no pressure to be hot.
Glad to have these breasts,
I celebrate not being a girl.

These legs were never meant to be hot.
Let others cheat with enhanced breasts.
In hindsight, what's scarier than being a girl?

POEM FOR THE PURCHASE OF A FIRST BRA

Let the older accompany the younger.
Let the older woman's purse be full
of salient things: sticks of gum to chew
to ease anxiety away, pretty postcards

of Swiss Alps to placate, distract,
an elegant pair of earrings, silver,
to anoint the younger woman's lobes.
Let the lighting in the store

be casual, kind, so soft that when
the younger woman disrobes, her body
fairly glows, surround by light
that does not disperse, will not fade.

Let the fitting room be empty
except for three women—the older,
the younger, the saleswoman who brings
various sizes on a velvet tray,

shutting curtains as she departs,
so older and younger can measure
in peace. Let everything be of silk,
the tape measure that spans

the girl's chest, the bras that will
not push or strafe. Let her choose
beyond black and white, let her
choose red, and purple, and blue.

Let the older adjust straps, seams,
make sure that nothing pinches
or twists, admiring the fit, fabric,
easing shoulders so the girl stands

erect, no slouch in her stance.
Let them choose together what suits.
Let the saleswoman wave goodbye,
ringing up no price tags this first time.

ELEGY FOR RICK JAMES

King of punk-funk, all braids
and swagger as your freaky girls
chanted in the background, choir
of unruly angels cooing,
hailing you—a nasty, sweaty,
spandex-wearing guitar slinger
who snorted and sucked and smoked
his fame away, glittering more than Bowie,
swaggering more than Elvis,
licking your lips at the kinky girls
who'd party all night long at
your bidding, hotel suites trashed,
virgins made sex-mad, lycra-clad.
My first record was a Rick James
record, and I had no idea
what that music could do
to my body, head, had no idea
what you meant when you sang
about six becoming nine,
your music stroking me in places
I didn't know I had, regions
far nastier than any I'd known,
slick, like the first time you see
a dirty magazine, that same rush.
Now I catch a picture of you
in *Rolling Stone*, braids gone,
face full, middle-aged,
your one good suit pressed
as you walk out of prison
and into that netherworld

of ex-celebrity, where no one
wants to hear the dozens of songs
you wrote in your prison cell.
Off the charts, you're persona
non grata, no Mary Jane Girls
or coked-up entourages awaiting
your licks and struts, your dance funk,
your music outrageous, your life an outrage.

O HOLY NIGHT

My father took a razor to the angel
that floated diaphanous atop our
Christmas tree, lopping its golden hair off
as lights fell from the tree's fake branches,
shards of colored glass glinting
in the carpet. He thundered about
Christmas—the white man's holiday—
as I trembled in the hallway,
out of sight, out of his mind.
There would be no singing today,
no hymns with "thee" and "thou,"
no praising a great white Father,
who would save us blacks from
our sinful essence, a burden
I could see every time he complained
about being called out of his name,
being made to feel less than a man.
He'd crossed oceans—from Grenada
to England, England to Canada—
crossed borders—Canada to the US—
all for nothing, all to be treated
like nothing. So no white angel
was going to mock him
in his own house, no matter
how much my mother tried
to pin his arms behind his back,
no matter how many angels lurked
above us, their skin pallid white,
their hair sinuous as wisteria.

Birth of a Nation

Our parents had to sign permission slips
to let us watch the greatest movie ever
made, D. W. Griffith's masterwork
of close-ups, carpetbaggers, magnolia
damsels, mouths open to scream
their silent fear of black brutes.
I sat tense at my desk, flickers of rage
curling my fingers as the film
reeled its images above: Negro "legislators"
crazed for chicken, dirty bare feet up
on desks as they chomped and gnawed
those bones, pale Flora jumping off
a cliff to escape a black man's touch.

I sat so tense no word, no joke
from my white, brainiac, whiz-kid friend
could soothe me, no lecture on historical
objectivity from my shrew-faced teacher
could calm the bitter at the back
of my throat. At that moment, in that
classroom, I wanted to know no white
people, to know nothing of this
long-dead white man who'd made

an ugliness this powerful, a shame
we didn't, wouldn't talk about.
How that classroom grew small
and hot and close, how conscious was I
of my black skin, mute, but not awed
like the audiences who cheered the halo
Griffith made float around a Klansman's head.

Where was my light, I wanted to ask,
who was going to glorify someone
like me? Certainly not my teacher,
who was only a woman, not a shrew,
not my friend the next desk over,
who was only a goofy kid good
at calculus. Who was going to build
a history from one lesson of despair,
one afternoon when all I could see
was that hooded figure projected above,
looming white and large, like a savior, a saint?

For My Brother

Brown-skinned baby, plump and happy,
your round dark eyes would follow
our father's every motion, his son
after two daughters, a boy to school
about fish and dirt, motors and grease.
You'd climb the furniture, laughing open-
mouthed, sticky fingerprints on Father's
rag-polished shoes. You'd have talks
I—being a girl and unskilled—was not
privy to—hours dismantling the lawn
mower, clanking it back together again.
But when you grew tall, when
your lanky form began to shift and stretch,
when you refused the calls of girls
who'd call just to hear if you'd speak
their names, when you spent more time
at the library than home, then suddenly
you weren't his boy anymore, dreaming
of college instead and the pleasure
of loving whomever, without fear of the belt
or the back of our father's hand.
You doodled boys' names in the margins
of your notebooks; plotted escapes from our
two-story dull brick house: scholarships,
internships, summer institutes upstate;
made me accomplice to plans I could
not tell. You dreamed until that day
Father stripped your room, found letters
to boys, not girls. He tore every page,
ripped your clothes from their hangers
as he shouted, shoving you down the stairs.

But none of this is true. You
don't exist, having never been born,
having never sworn me to secrecy
over love for a boy two desks away.
Why then, can I see your face,
tearful and twisted as my father
ripped up your clothes and books;
why then, can I hear his rage
destroying you, pushing you
down the stairs, out of my life?

SOME OF MY BEST FRIENDS ARE WHITE PEOPLE

When Katie said, *And when you told the audience,*
'my husband's here,' everyone in that all-white place
turned around to find the black man there,
I knew that my secret weapons against racism
were my white friends themselves, my beloved race traitors.
That audience assumed that my husband had to be black,
because I'm black, and clearly proud to be so . . .
The assumptions go on and on, and most times,
it's my white friends who can see them, critique them.
I'm so used to assumptions based on my color
that they don't register anymore; like static on a television screen,
they're there, but I ignore them. So I shouldn't be startled
when my husband detects rudeness I don't hear,
not surprised when Carolyn's shocked when we
are led to a back-of-the-room table at Denny's
after forty minutes. My friends remind me
not to be used to it when some remark slips out
of some other white mouth, that this is not business
as usual. But it's business in America, a country
where I can't afford the price of my own vigilance,
monitoring the toll of racism too big a job for just one race.

HEADSTONE

My father's body lies beneath the stone;
my mother lies beneath him in her box.
Their faces fade from memory. I know
them less and less each day. I try
to see what they have left behind
in us: my sister's face like his, like hers,
my laugh a family's laugh I listen for.
I save the little pieces of their lives.

My mother lies beneath him in her box.
We kept her purses full, but touch
them less and less each day. I try
to call my father's presence up
in us, my sister's face like his, like hers,
like minds, like limbs. I kept the tag—
I save the little pieces of their lives—
the ID tag from luggage he would use.

We kept her purses full, but touch
their contents less and less, no time
to call my mother's presence up,
to finger cancelled bank receipts, pay stubs.
Like minds, like limbs. I kept the tag
embossed with his—with our—address,
the ID tag from luggage he would use,
plastic, colored fake like burnished gold.

Their contents less and less. No time.
My laugh a family's laugh I listen for.
To finger cancelled bank receipts, pay stubs,

to see what they have left behind,
embossed with his—with our—address.
Their faces fade from memory, I know,
to plastic, colored fake like burnished gold.
My father's body lies beneath the stone.

After Shaving My Head, I Begin to Think Beauty Is Overrated

Why, why, why goes the anguished refrain of friends,
as if I'd shaved their heads instead of my own.

Some are clearly repelled—women are supposed to have hair,
and here I've gone and shaved my head cleaner than an

NBA player's, my scalp tender, brown and bright, able now
to pick up frequencies of cold it's never felt before.

Is this a political statement? one colleague asks;
I think you look better with a little bit of hair, one blunt

student declares. When I explain I'd only wanted to know
how it felt to be able to glide hands over scalp with

nothing impeding the motion, no one's satisfied.
Surely this gesture means something—maybe my marriage

is failing, or I'm suicidal, looking for ways to strike back,
get even with a culture that prizes women's hair more

than women's lives. It's only when my husband says,
It might not grow back the same way,

do I feel the slightest panic. But I can't be mad at him.
When I emerged from the bathroom, head half-shaven,

arms aching from scraping a ladies' disposable razor
across my scalp, he looked at me, sighed,

and said, *If you're going to do this,*
let's do this right, taking his can of shaving cream

from his travel bag, spraying a thick layer
of dense foam all over my unfinished head.

Confessions of a Barefaced Woman

Befuddled by makeup's odd apparatus,
I feel too strange in it—coated, shellacked,
primped to a version of myself I can't wait

to wash off, letting bare skin breathe.
Clumsy with twisted mascara brushes
that look like screws dipped in soot,

I fumble to draw lines with brow pencils
that come with miniature sharpeners
whose blades shave each pencil to dangerous

points. Lipstick has never felt right—
too waxy and thick, so heavy I'm always tempted
to wipe it off, smear it across my face

like a girl caught playing at her mother's
vanity table. Face powder makes me cough
and sneeze, rouge makes me look as if

I've slapped my cheeks with big red circles,
a refugee from circus college. Some women
know those secrets of color, precise

geometries that entice in russet and bronze,
gold and ruby, deep brooding colors
over lips, under arched brows, on lids.

I'll admire their artistry from a distance,
know wrinkles I never learned to mask
will etch their paths across my forehead,

around my eyes and mouth,
no second skin for me to wipe away
at day's end, nothing to reveal.

A History of African-American Hair

Ghosts of hairstyles past visit me in the mirror:
pageboy bangs like Tootie's on *The Facts of Life*,

black power braids aping Stevie Wonder, not
Bo Derek, Afro puffs that sprouted from each

side of my head, neat tracks of cornrows tight
across my scalp, curling iron flips, top knots,

pigtails, blow-dried hair, hot-combed hair,
permed hair, straightened-with-Vigorol hair—

a shampoo so noxious that exposing
any other body part to it was to court

chemical burns. I remember the knots, snags,
tangles—my normally patient mother cursing

as she tried to pull a comb through
just-washed hair, a mass dense as a forest,

just as resistant. I remember the goopy gels,
greasy lotions, pressing oils and pomades,

cans of hairspray and mousse, the barrettes,
bobby pins, end papers, metal clips,

head scarves, doo rags, hair dryer bonnets,
pink sponge curlers, hard wire curlers,

big plastic curlers with rows of holes
shot through them, straightening combs,

crimping irons, blow dryers with their
toothy attachments. All that junk

would crowd around the bathroom sink,
under it, under my bed, sofa, arm chair.

I remember and I am glad as any woman can be
that I cut my hair, that the woman in the mirror

now has hair she can touch,
cropped close to scalp, to skin.

To Be Young, Not-So-Gifted, and Black

The thing that makes you exceptional, if you are at all,
is inevitably that which must also make you lonely.
—Lorraine Hansberry

On an evaluation, a student complains:
I wouldn't have taken this class
had I known all we were going to read
was black poetry! I check the syllabus,
find two black poets: Harper, Hayden.
I hadn't even included a black woman.
Was it my black face that student hated,
my lips turning every poem into black poetry,
into what so offended him or her that poetry
was now forever spoiled? Then I think,
What would Lorraine do?—Hansberry
so elegant and poised in her Capri pants and sweaters,
face so alive with intelligence it comes through
even in these small photos in her paperback
autobiography. I bet she'd have something
coolly trenchant to say, and she'd say it
so wittily that student would want to be black,
to be that much closer to conquering Broadway,
capturing critics. Hansberry would have
just the right answer, just the right
ironic distance, putting it on stage,
making the protagonist more interesting
than I am, far more adept but conflicted, too,
audience watching her every scene, act.
I'm just a year younger than Lorraine was
when she died. The lump in my breast

is benign, hers wasn't. The words I reach for
are untested, unscripted, unsettled.
Lorraine's words make this burden of black
something I can handle as I add more
black names to the syllabus, more chances
for the people who will always hate my skin
to hate it even more, learn less.

The Reluctant Integrationist

She is the woman who wears kente cloth
to a Congressional hearing, her African headwrap
shining out among blue suits and power ties.

She's tired of requests to touch her dreads/
braids/curls/kinks/'fro/twists, of being
a living example during Black History Month

only, wants to be heard year-round instead.
She wants a life that's done with firsts:
first degree in the family, first letter

in her personnel files citing "lack of collegiality"
and "dubious research." She wants to stop
the tenure clock, to see another brown face

hired, though reluctant to lay that burden down
at another's feet. Tell her something good,
know her first name, meet her for coffee

and ask her anything except how it feels
to be the one representing the race
in the narrow commerce of academic hallways,

the silent labs, classrooms. Let her tell you
in her own time, her own where and when,
moments with you among the few

when she isn't talented tenth,
not statistic or percentage,
but person, woman, lover

of Sunday morning jazz brunches,
coldest champagne and cinnamon,
of anything powerfully brown.

GRACE JONES AT THE REPUBLICAN NATIONAL CONVENTION

All the delegates cease
their star-spangled
conversations when she,

lycra-clad, spike-heeled,
slinks onto the floor,
lady delegates from Texas

fainting at the sight
of her. Black woman
fierce in leopard skin,

fur-lined studded
collars, angles of
her cut so bristle-

sharp that delegates
from Iowa wonder
just what barber

she goes to. No
straw hat knows
just who she's calling

darling, her biceps
better than anyone's
here, stronger than

tonight's platform.
Surveying this affair's
lack of fashion sense,

she casts doubt on pins
in red, white and blue,
such colors are so

through. Stroking
her shoulders, thighs,
she raises her regal

dark head, growls,
then says, *Did not
anyone tell you,*

*I'm here to sing
your anthem?* as a
mirrored ball descends,

strobes bathing her
in light, open mouths
agape from fifty states.

THE OTHER ALLISON

Leo, my courtesy van driver,
wants to know my name.
I tell him Allison,
and he tells of an Allison
he knew and loved and almost married,
a good-for-nothing woman
who laid up in his house
for two years, smoking weed all day
while dishes piled up,
The house so nasty, Leo says,
I didn't hardly recognize it.
Leo don't do no drugs, he claims,
and I almost laugh, delighted
to think of this indolent woman
whom I love already,
imagining her luxuriant
in robe and curlers, painting
her nails while Leo slaves
for minimum wage at some job
where he grins like a Pullman porter—
Yes, sir and *No, sir* all day.
I imagine her stunning—
skin the color of rich cocoa,
Dorothy Dandridge smile,
legs so long and dangerous
Leo loves her despite himself,
despite words from his good mama.
I want to be this Allison,
not the humdrum woman I am
who listens politely to strangers,

hoping to use what she hears.
I want to be the kind of woman
who makes industrious men
lose their minds, though I never
lift a finger, cook a meal,
wash a plate.

Leo tells me he had to cut her loose,
and now Allison lives on the streets,
brothers chiding him for putting
a sister that fine out of his house.
Is this just a tale, something
Leo weaves and reweaves to pass
each trip from airport to hotel
and back, fiction to make me press
a tip in his palm when the ride's done?
When Leo asks, *So what do you do?*
I say, *I get up in the morning,*
I teach. He nods, but I know he wants
me to say, *You're full of it,*
there was no Allison, we Allisons
are too hardworking for that.
As he drops me at the hotel,
I wonder how the tale
will be different for the next
passenger, if each woman's name
has its own story.

VACATIONS

It feels so lovely to dream of them
while sitting at your desk at work,
typing another blessed memo no one
will read, tossing your paragraphs
into the recycle bin though they're hot
off the copy machine. It is lovely
to dream of the rarefied oxygen
of mountaintop elevations,
of the assiduous sun over white sand
beaches unspoiled by medical waste
or municipal garbage. For weeks,
you think of nothing but those
two weeks—planning your meals
and outfits, calling your travel agent
on the sly to see if she can get you
one more ticket for your brother's
wife's sister's son, who's back
from rehab and in need of a little
family interaction. Or is that intervention?
No matter. These two sparkling weeks
can't be spoiled by an unexpected
teenage boy in love with sulkiness
and H. You're going to wear that fuchsia
swimsuit; you're going to line up
at admissions booths for local attractions,
handing your dollars to the bored girl
behind the counter; you're going
to walk around, dopey tourist,
binoculars around your neck,
broad-brimmed hat, goofy as a

dunce cap, perched on your head.
And if your rental car starts to shake
on that mountain incline, and if
the amusement park is closed due
to an *E. coli* outbreak, and if someone
steals your wallet, plane ticket, and
credit cards, you'll still be dazed
with the promise of what a vacation's
supposed to be—happy people on brochures
sliding down water chutes or tramping
about on horseback; couples, tanned all over,
lying on a deserted beach; little kids
biting bright red watermelon slices.
And you'll start planning for next year
before you're even back at your desk
again, before the Xerox copier
has a chance to break down once more.

Ex-New Yorkers

complain about the coffee in Cleveland,
the newspaper in Little Rock,
the pretzels in Philadelphia,
the Chinese food in Columbus.
Ex-New Yorkers will kill you
for a same-day copy of the *New York Times*,
will explain to you that what passes for pizza
in Chicago won't pass muster in Brooklyn.

Never see a movie set in New York
with an ex-New Yorker. They will prattle on
about locations, proclaim that the movie's characters
can't be in Harlem one moment, Greenwich Village
the next, explicating each plot point
by saying, *That couldn't happen in New York*,
that real New York criminals don't wear Armani,
unless they work for the Securities and Exchange Commission.

Ex-New Yorkers think Central Park
is the greatest city park in the world,
forgetting its zoo full of forlorn animals
in rusting cages. Ex-New Yorkers
won't ever tell that they never
actually went to MoMA or the Met,
even when the Picasso exhibit came through.

Never offer an ex-New Yorker a bagel.
Or a knish. Or a hot dog. Don't make
their eyes roll with vacation memories
of Wollman ice rink at Christmas time

or your sojourn to see the Rockettes
at Radio City. Such bourgeois pleasures
only make an ex-New Yorker yawn.

To mollify an ex-New Yorker, listen.
Listen as they talk of Chinatown
and Little Italy, Flushing Meadows Park
and Yankee Stadium, the FDR Drive
and the West Side Highway. Listen
as they extol the pleasures of crowded
subways, crowded buses, crowded sidewalks
and crowded apartments. Do not,
under any circumstances, mention Boston.

The Aisles of Misfit Equipment

We purchase each item with best intentions:
stair stepper, its endless climbing endlessly boring,
stationary bike that took us nowhere but our own
freezing basements, dumbbells that mock us

with their name. Self-improvement seems so easy
when each piece of equipment is shiny-clean,
showroom bright, the perfect body attainable
on credit. Only minutes a day at home

and we'll be ready to compete
for Ms. Fitness America, dropping
dress sizes like bad boyfriends.
But minutes a day becomes minutes

every other day, then minutes once a week,
until the only things stationary are us,
waists widening so dramatically
the best discipline becomes none at all,

the bike put in turnaround at Play It Again Sports,
a store dedicated to the proposition that all
overzealous exercisers will come to their senses—
trade in the rowers for badminton sets,

iron weights for mini trampolines.
We keep working our way down,
working out less and less until some blood test
decrees we visit these aisles, buy back

what we sold off. Doctor's orders this time,
we lace our grubby sneakers, knowing how
gluttony can slow the blood, make
lungs labor for every costly breath.

THE VAGINA BUSINESS

He said he wasn't in the vagina business!
—Emma Thompson as Maggie in *Peter's Friends*

For years, I had no clue
what you looked like,
though I'd read the feminist pamphlets
calling you a wet flower,
gazed at textbook illustrations
revealing mechanisms as intricate
as a Swiss watch's workings.
It wasn't right, I thought,
to see you bare in daylight,
exposed so men could defeat you
with sullen nomenclature—gash,
slit, snatch. Sure, I'd touched you,
but thought it didn't count
as long as I was face down,
pillow smothering sighs.
What a day it was
when I summoned the courage
to really look at you—one hand
holding the mirror, the other parting
fold from fold. You glistened
a welcome, revealed at further touch
pleasures far sturdier than flowers.
Your business is one of accommodation,
adaptation, and I must admit I admire
your flexibility, the way you take in
a finger, two fingers, five inches.
Nowadays I don't need to see you

to praise you, all I need to do
is stroke the small hot center
guarding your inner gates
and I'm enchanted all over again
by your grand ambitions, slick response.

In Praise of the Penis

Funny little fellow,
all our slang for you
is harsh—prick, dick, cock—
hard consonants erupting
from our mouths, jutting like
the bulge on the school jock.
But usually you're quite
harmless, sleepy as a baby
and just as needy.
You're quite laughable, really—
rod, tool, yardstick—I don't care
what you call yourself,
how you glorify your shape
and/or size, you'll forever
seem to me to be some sort
of elevated inchworm,
a fleshy extraterrestrial
from late night sci-fi—
instead of *The Blob*,
my marquee reads *The Penis*—
mobs of screaming virgins,
clad in knee socks and angora,
run to escape a creature
who's come to life in 3-D,
threatening the town's very virtue.
Most undignified fellow,
I won't leave your care
to anyone else, won't
replace you with some toy
bought from the back of a magazine.

You fascinate me, though
I've seen your act before—
the humble slow awakenings,
firecracker finishes. Still,
I'm always glad when you
decide to let loose once more,
spilling on newly-washed sheets
until you're weary, bashful, spent.

Venus de Milo Takes a Sexual Enlightenment for Women Class

All her life she's heard whispers about it, and now
that she's a real live woman, free from posing, arms intact,
she signs up at the Learning Annex for a one-night-only
seminar called "Female Pleasure: The Final Frontier."
Being Roman, she doesn't really know what a frontier is,
but imagines it as vast and flat as a huge palm,
an open space so blank her voice echoes.
In the classroom she enters all she can see
are four other women, looking post-work tired,
businesswomen in suits, sneaker-clad. They eye
her toga, suspicious of any woman who wears anything
that loose. Their guide to sexual frontier wears
a sweatshirt with the word "Michigan" on it,
and Venus wonders if that's the name of a god
she's never heard of. The women all talk at once:
He never touches me there, all I want is some foreplay,
I hate that getting down on my knees. Foreplay?
Knees? Their words hold mysteries for Venus,
silent as she stares at the women in cheerless suits.
When the woman with Michigan on her chest spots Venus,
she's elated, crows, *Stand up, stand up. Now here,*
she says, pointing at Venus, *is a woman in charge*
of her sexuality! Look at her and learn to love your body!

NAPE

Smart men don't wear ties.
They know the neck exists
to be caressed, the nape
a haunt for lips throughout
the night, hollow at the base
of the throat just right for
one slim finger to stroke.
How soft the skin beneath
the chin, how vulnerable.
And I like the jut
of the chin itself, bone hard
under my wayward fingers.
So don't cover what I want
so much to touch, lose
the flimsy flags of fabric,
be brave enough to show
the path that leads to all
the places I like even better.
Smart men know where
my hands will always start
their search, and they'll never
be caught wasting time
undoing tight slip knots
when there are better ways
to spend those potent minutes.

WHY MEN WHISTLE

Maybe some chemical inside their brains
makes them behave this way: hooting
as they drive slowly by, whistling sharp

and long as they check out whatever's
coming: women assessed at a glance.
Maybe they need to be heard in three

states, and that's why they're yelling,
Whoop, there it is, pointing out the
obvious, selecting targets. But why

do they slow for me, undistinguished
in a dark turtleneck, jeans, a sweater
your grandmother might wear? Why stop

to peer at a woman with an
unpainted face and unprocessed hair,
nothing done to change drab to daring,

no skin showing. Still, they drive slowly
when they see me alone, wanting
to know if I'm married, happily so,

asking to give me a ride to wherever
I'm going, hoping to take me places
only they know about. I tell them

I like to walk, that my husband's expecting
me soon, that I don't get into strange
cars. And that chemical in their brains

clicks off as they drive by, realizing
I'm not worth the time, or money,
or effort when there are too many

others to stop, better-looking women
who'll want a ride to the club only they
know about, a place too far to reach on foot.

ON VIEWING TWO DIFFERENT DATE RAPE MOVIES

Both movies star actresses better known
for playing daughters on sitcoms,
faces familiar as students you once had,
or girls you knew yourself in college.
Each movie begins with a raucous frat party
filled with beer-guzzling white boys
(though each frat has its token non-white)
who ambush young women because
they're there, which must mean they want it,
they're asking for it. In both movies
the former sitcom daughters drink
far more than they can handle
then stumble into a room to escape
the swilling throngs, passing out
only to find their boyfriend's best friend
or their older brother's best friend
on top, thrusting in. But here's where
the movies part—the made-for-TV one
starring that round-faced girl from *Full House*
is so violent you can't mistake this act
for anything else—he rips her clothes,
ignores her screams, thrusts so hard
she can't move, and when he's done,
she runs off crying, trying to cover herself,
blouse torn. In the theatrical movie,
the redheaded daughter from *Kate & Allie*
lies there stunned, passed out,
makeshift toga baring stark skin.
When he mounts her, her cries are faint,
tired, but she doesn't fight, protest mumbled

until he's all the way inside, and her face
reveals just where he's invaded, how far.
All the while he coos about her beauty.
Which is the version to believe?
Which actress is more wounded,
more authentic? Which one looks
like a favorite niece or your best student
from two semesters ago
who sat weeping in your office
for no reason she would name?
When do these stop being movies
and start being something you catch
on their faces, shoulders, checking
for scratches when you're taking roll,
hoping each Monday learning can happen
after the weekend, the parties,
the encounters you're never privy to?

JANIS JOPLIN VISITS CHEERLEADING CAMP

How dare you take my songs,
blast them out to the world,
then make up little routines—
precious steps, turns, tossing
sleek hair back to mock my frizz,
your sneakers and shirts matching,
skin burnished, suntan bright.
I'd like to take a piece
of each one of your hearts,
ripping them out so you know
how it feels to be voted
ugliest man on campus when
you're a girl from Port Arthur, Texas,
the kind of girl shunned during
proms, parades, tailgates, hayrides.
You girls don't know the howl
I hear in my head is Bessie's howl,
a black woman's sound coming out
of a white woman's mouth,
unruly growls your mothers would not love,
calling me dirty, not worth a dime.
I'm worth a whole lot more dead
than you all are alive, voice stronger
than all yours together, my clothes
the clothes you are silly enough
to pay big money for, calling them
your slumming clothes—velvet,
swirling cascades of scarves and beads,
fringe and feathers you play in,
not knowing their passion, power.

The world called me Pearl,
what will it call you?

ROLE MODELS

The next time a man demands to know
who my literary foremothers are, I want
to see his jaw drop when I say, straight-

faced, Wonder Woman, the Bionic Woman,
and Supergirl. I want to see him nod politely
when I reveal my childhood's pivotal moment—

watching Lynda Carter chase crooks in a red,
white and blue bustier, fighting crime and
busting Nazis with bullet-repellent bracelets

and her golden lasso of truth. I loved how
she'd spin around, transform from mousy
military secretary into a well-endowed crusader

for justice and the common good. Even
my father commented approvingly: *That woman
sure has some big lungs*, he'd say, admiring

cleavage that bobbed as she pursued the baddest
of bad guys. She even piloted an invisible plane,
had a whole island of Amazonian sisters for back-up.

That's very nice, my companion will say, shying away
during this reverie, leaving me alone to ponder
the Bionic Woman and Supergirl, their places in the canon

less secure, their derivation from male heroes.
Still, all three made me want to fly, and what's more feminist
than challenging who can take off, who stays bound to the ground?

DAUGHTER, MOTHER, SISTER, WIFE

When your daughter is a poet,
burn all your possessions before you die.
Or else she will riffle through them,
searching for that one bauble, that trinket,
that one letter or card or bus schedule
to explain why you were so cold, so reluctant
to pick her up when she was nine,
when she was nineteen. Burn all
your correspondence; but be warned,
she'll make something of the cinders.

When your mother is a poet,
your breakfast may be marmalade
and wine, wheat toast and dandelion
stems. She may slit a fish's belly open
in a gesture so sudden and swift
that you can never eat fish again,
her eyes gleaming with conquest.
When your mother is a poet,
you may get crumpets, not pizza,
gravy but no potatoes.
You may not get fed at all.

When your sister is a poet,
she may steal your stories
for her own, her life's humiliations
not nearly as intriguing as yours.
She'll become the one whose left breast
popped out of her prom gown;
she'll be the one with the extra-smarmy

94

dentist, the one at your father's
graveside, mother's deathbed.
She will send these words off to strangers,
and not discuss one page of it with you.

When your wife is a poet,
watch your mouth. Anything you say
can and will be used, anything you do
preserved whether you think it should be
or not. She may quit being your wife,
but she will never quit searching her memory
for that awful thing you said
in the delivery room, the laundry room,
the bedroom, the kitchen.
And she will write it down
in that penmanship you always loved—
an ornate script that looked
like another era's handiwork,
malice controlled by curves
and loops in ink, swelling on paper.

WHAT WOMEN WANT

More women have done this than you can imagine,
proclaim the scribes at *Playboy*, opulent affairs
with one another, seemingly straight women
desiring other women for reasons these writers
kindly explain to their readers, those men
who have everything, or at least, like to think
they do. *Women want passion*, the article says,
they have needs men can't satisfy—
smaller, defter hands, more delicate and patient,
softer lips that don't delve too deep,
hips that don't move or feel like male hips,
hair on them finer, easier on the tongue.
One woman they interview reveals:
There's more give and take with a woman,
less divide and conquer, plus I was tired
of giving head—tired of sore knees.
The men at *Playboy* knew sisterhood was powerful,
but not this powerful, and I wonder if they wonder
if their Playmates have been doing each other,
those centerfolds more unattainable than previously
suspected. *If you're worried about your girlfriend,*
they caution, *watch for these signs—*a certain
languor, a sudden comfort in her own skin,
a confused stare at your most seductive grin.
The ones who are truly lesbians probably won't
come back, they lament, *but don't panic,*
most of them drift back to the other side.
I don't want to love a side, I want to love
a person, a person who doesn't fret
over where my hands have been, whose nipples

I have kissed, whose legs I have parted
in search of who I could taste, love.

Bad Meals Threaten Our Marriage

I'm not afraid you'll leave me,
tempted by the wily charm
of some long-legged adulteress,
or that one day, while you're driving,
the car will spin out on a patch of ice,
send you careening through
the splintering windshield.
But I am afraid we'll argue ourselves
past consternation and into divorce court
if we fight over one more meal—
what to eat, where to eat it,
how low to settle in a town
where Ponderosa is the steakhouse ideal,
Denny's for after-dinner dessert splendor.
Our desires exceed our surroundings,
our cravings not sated at Burger King,
especially one that reeks
of the most cloying disinfectant,
breeding an unfortunate synthesis
of textures, tastes, aromas.
I don't ever want another pizza
if it has to come from Godfather's,
an offer anyone with taste buds
can refuse. Shoney's always surprises—
one day, no hot water, another day, no cold.
Even the diner, packed late nights
with studying throngs, serves lousy
diner food—the chicken soup bereft
of noodles, tasting of off-color lemons.
You claim the burgers at our campus McDonald's

aren't made of real beef, speculate that's the reason
our students are grey-faced, gaunt.

Too tired to cook, too tired to fight,
too tired to drive around any longer,
we head to the supermarket,
grab boxes of Klondike bars
and plastic tubs of sherbet—
lemon-lime or mango-peach more exotic
than any franchised fare.
This may be the first marriage
saved by frozen foods,
by the small consolations
of prepackaged meals,
bad food, for sure, but at least
we didn't pick it up at
a drive-thru, at least
we'll add water and stir
in our own kitchen.

FLIRTATION

I like my tights electric blue,
my shoes of patent leather.
This dance I dance is meant for you—
I move quick as new weather.

My shoes of patent leather
shine brighter than my skin.
I move, quick as new weather,
to shed the dress I'm in.

Shining brighter than my skin,
my eyes, they say it all.
I'll shed the dress I'm in,
let summer fabric fall.

My eyes, they see it all.
They see what's false, what's true.
Let summer fabric fall.
I know what we can do.

I know what's false, what's true.
I dance the dance that's meant for you.
Show me what you can do.
You like my tights, electric blue.

JUNK FOOD

One day I nearly cracked my skull wide open,
feet flying out from under as I fell
down a series of slate stone steps
iced over by Indiana winter
because I had to have a bag of Oreos.
I didn't care that ice was everywhere,
that my breath hung, a frozen vapor.
I wanted to lick that creamy white middle,
let its sugar dissolve all over my tongue
and teeth, to crunch those round
black cookies, savoring them with a glass
of milk colder than the air outside.
Fool for sweetness, I would have
run out naked had there been free bags
tossed in the snow, bounty from a jackknifed
Nabisco truck. No substitute would do,
no supermarket brand or nearest competitor—
I wanted no other crumbs on my lips, fingers,
table. So when I roused myself,
dazed from the fall, the cold,
my head a heavy weight that bumped
all three steps on the way down,
I still craved a taste sweeter
than anything upstairs in the house,
a certainty even winter couldn't kill.

Dinner Party

No late-night candles flicker here, no resonant sax notes linger,
No Glenlivet is poured into whisky tumblers, no china,

gold-edged, graces our battered dining room table. I'm wishing
for shrimp cocktail, salacious brie, duck roasted savory-tender,

but what we're having tonight is straight from the can:
chicken noodle, turkey rice, minestrone. I'm wishing

I could be as gorgeous as a Carnival dancer in Rio,
shimmying to percolating Brazilian rhythms in a dress

so short, so tight, that you'd have to guess where it ends,
where I begin. But I've been in the same nightgown

for three days, your hair's askew from tossing
in flu-tormented sleep, sweat beading your t-shirt.

Forget gardenias for my hair, forget cufflinks
for your sleeves, forget replicating the clever banter

of famous movie couples—Bogie, Bacall, Nick
and Nora Charles. I bet you Fred and Ginger

never had to dance around a movie set
with coughing this persistent and insidious

nagging at their chests. Bleary, sleep-deprived,
I wouldn't call this romance with any other partner,

even as you turn away when I offer the smallest
kiss. *Contagious love*, you tease, and offer me

orange juice and Vitamin C instead,
sipping from another steaming bowl

you hope will cure what ails, what keeps us
without passion, separate, aching, chilled.

Why I'm Not a Scholar

I've never been able to talk that diction,
and let's face it, who likes those clothes?
I shudder to think of a life giving papers,
and though I think I'm sufficiently smart,
I've never been the scholarly journal type.
Nothing scares me more than doctoral degrees.

I barely made it through my own degree—
the scary academic jargon, diction
I hated to spell and type.
I'd be at my desk, in grungy clothes,
lamenting that I wasn't smart,
fearing an incomplete on another paper.

When I finally turned in those papers,
they returned ink-covered to such a degree,
I thought that I was surely losing my smarts.
One teacher scrawled, *Improve your diction!*
and I thought, *Yeah when you improve your clothes!*
As students go, I wasn't her type.

Perhaps I should have paid someone to type,
research the facts on all those papers.
But my lies would have been unclothed,
I was never good at lying to that degree.
So I went on grappling with MLA diction,
believing I would never be as smart

as "true" academics—now they were smart.
You know, the bookish quiet types

who never speak in normal diction?
They always seem to be presenting a paper.
I fear they'll hit me with rolled-up degrees,
index cards spilling from their clothes.

I recognize authentic scholars by their clothes—
ensembles that once were smart
in the year they finished their last degree.
OK, it's cruel of me to stereotype—
scholars, too, get up, read the morning paper,
too bleary-eyed to judge faulty diction.

Even if I managed the diction, I'd hate the clothes,
and if I gave a paper that wasn't smart,
I'd probably meet types who'd demand my degree.

It Wasn't a Love Connection

Better get out of that funk, girlfriend,
fix your hair and brush your teeth.
Don't let no greasy-haired romeo
make you feel so bad about yourself
that you can't get out of bed.
I know he stood you up, left you
waiting in the bar while he watched
the NFL or NBA or some such thing,
and I know you are tired of trifling
men with their pleadings, excuses,
and outright lies. You have got
to get yourself together, do justice
to the body and brain God gave you
in her infinite wisdom. That's right,
I said her, 'cause if God were a man
don't you think he would have made men
just a little bit more celestial?
She's testing us, see, making us
stronger through tribulation.
These men round here are trouble,
but little do they know that when
both sexes get up to those ivory gates,
God will have all their lies and deceits
on videotape, newest technology and everything.
So get up, wash your face, and put on
that blouse you look so good in.
We're going out to turn down
all the Mr. Pitifuls that come our way,
divine providence clearly on our side.

THE IDEAL LISTENER

All poets want me at their readings.
I laugh—appropriately—at their jokes,
not a raucous guffaw, but not
an embarrassed titter, either—smile
as an adroit turn of phrase leaves
a writer's lips, lingers in the air,
settles in the mind. I'm attentive
during the sad poems, face downcast
but not cast down, fingers not fidgeting
for want of something better to do.
And I'm nonjudgmental during
the erotic poems, discreetly not
imagining the poet's body as the body
intent on all those sexy acrobatics.
I don't get up, not even for a sip
of water or a bathroom break,
unless I have the slightest hint
of a cough that would have me
making noise when there should
be silence, except for the funny parts,
when there should be laughter.
I am so good at what I do
that poets should rent me out,
pay me each time I settle into
some uncomfortable seat, their books
in my hands as I follow along word
for word, every poem one more chance
to show us all how this should be done.

HOMAGE TO LEONARDO DREW'S *NUMBER 8*

—Installation, St. Louis Art Museum

So this is your art, a black man's art,
this mass hanging from ceiling to floor,
this rage of tattered ropes, bird carcasses,
burnt feathers molting in steely cargo.
I can't ignore this ugliness you've turned
inside out, anger made palpable—
coiled cords of sooty rope twining around
raccoon and porcupine skulls, animal hides
and antlers torn, fractured shards in this
assemblage, wood ruptured in it too,
the whole heft of it black, painted black—
the ripped rags, deer bones. What
made you build this? What drove you
to salvage the accidents others spurn,
turn them into this dense wall no one
can pass by, turn from? Uncomprehending,
I stop and breathe a hard breath
before your amalgam of rope, wood, paint,
your loom of blistered discards.

I Love You, Jimmy Poquette

was scrawled on the dollar bill the cashier handed me
when she gave me my change. Just who was Jimmy,
I wondered, and why would a girl sign his name
on a dollar in hopes he would see it?
I know it's a girl 'cause it's that sort
of handwriting—loopy, confessional, ninth grade.
Is Jimmy the king of the ninth grade—swaggering
through the schoolyard, baggy jeans sagging
off one bony hip, hair falling into his eyes
so he constantly has to run his hands through it?
Is he the sort of boy too beautiful for his age—
smooth-skinned, fair-haired, eyes girls whisper
about when they think they're in love?
I wonder what Jimmy Poquette did
when he found this dollar—did he throw it
back in the face of the girl who claimed
to love him, that shy girl who sits in back
during history class, the one so awkward
she seems to be falling down when she's
standing up? Did he pocket the note saying
nothing, refusing to look that girl
in the face, afraid he might feel something
finer than pity? Or did he take the dollar,
go straight to the grocery, use it to buy
a pack of smokes, so he could pose outside
the high school, a cigarette he never lights
hanging from between his lips, lips
every freshman girl has dreamed about,
soft, firm, red and wettened by his tongue?

BALLADE FOR DOROTHY PARKER

Some only know your sharp Algonquin wit,
the only woman writer at the Table.
Your satire could cover ugly splits—
those love affairs gone wrong. Unstable,
drinking through the Twenties, you weren't able
to stay away from men, those savages.
They called you humorist. You hated the label.
Four suicide attempts, three marriages.

You shucked your father's name, with it
your Jewish heritage, woman unable
to hold her tongue. *Vanity Fair* made you quit,
your play reviews too harsh—no fables
of the feminine for you, no mink and sable
mindset. You wrote out damages
in verse, hiding despair in labor.
Four suicide attempts, three marriages.

No housewife you, not a woman content to knit,
you joined the Loyalists in Spain, enabled
the Screen Actors Guild, wrote movies to outwit
the status quo, mocked gents and neighbors,
society matrons and dandies disabled
by portraits of their greed. Miscarriages
of justice made you braver.
Four suicide attempts, three marriages.

Dorothy, you found so little you could savor.
One husband's suicide stopped that remarriage.
At seventy-five, your heart gave out, belabored.
Four suicide attempts. Three marriages.

Misery: A Guide

First, allow resentments to build
for as long as possible, decades
if you can manage it. Blame
everyone else for your troubles:
your insulting father, manic
mother, your severe sixth-grade
teacher. File away all misdeeds,
mull over every slight until
you're sure the world was set
against you from birth, no turn
of the karmic wheel able
to set your life right. Give up
your quest for the perfect mate, job,
stay with whatever jerk makes you
most weepy, your office a cubicle
with no ventilation or warmth.
Make lists of all the people
who've ever let you down:
your first lover, your second,
that snotty girl sophomore year
who delighted in cackling
at your hair, your clothes.
Get so far in debt that you
could never pay it off in one
lifetime, credit record so soiled
no bank will loan you money
to replace your clunking car.
Accept no responsibility, wash
your hands of this life and expect
nothing from the next, content

that your misery was all your own
making, the one thing no one
could ever take away, a malevolence
so thorough no solace or prayer
could have reached you, nothing
possible but life's darkest underside,
dimmest corridors of rage.

The Liars

How I admire their skills,
their easy way with oratory:
the phrases, full of promises

that trip from their tongues
and into the public's ears,
their finesse at sharing

life's most intimate details
without stammering, stumbling—
loves lost, damage suffered,

homes they owned, then lost,
cars they cherished, then crashed.
They narrate every detail

without flinching, crying,
so swift in their stories
everything you thought was true

blurs, right and wrong
shifting in and out of focus.
It's not that they mean

to be dishonest, after all,
everyone lies, and some
are just better at it

than others, some have the gift
that enables them to glide
where others break down,

to remain placid while others,
nonplussed, cannot figure out
the deceptions they've woven,

unable to remember
the logic of their lies.
I wish I could be one

of them, so proficient
at making the world bend
to my desires, but I haven't

the skills, the patience,
haven't been a believable liar
since sixth grade when I lied

my way out of boring homework
by telling my hapless teacher
I was a slave at home—cooking,

cleaning, washing every dish.
When I was found out,
I couldn't sit for a week,

the lies beat out of me
by my stern father,
who, incidentally,

made his living from lies,
selling one new product
after another, always claiming

this new version worked best.
I should have learned from him
how to sell something not

worth selling, should have
learned to sell myself
just as he sold himself—

lying right into everyone's
good graces with his smile,
speech, his absolute certainty

that everything he sold,
every word he uttered was
worth the cost, guaranteed.

Regrets

I should be watching my weight, counting calories,
　　　doing leg lifts and squat thrusts, but instead I'm under
　　　six layers of thermal blankets, watching
　　　Saturday morning cartoons featuring
　　　robots that look like animals
or animals that look like robots.
I should be writing letters on custom-made stationery,
　　　engaging notes to long-lost friends—
　　　high school buddies, college pals—
　　　instead of reading gossip on the Internet
　　　about celebrities I'll never meet
　　　and don't really like.
I should be doing something productive in life:
　　　writing better poems, cooking exotic cuisines—
　　　but instead I'm eating noodles from a Styrofoam cup,
　　　doodling in the margins
　　　of blank notebooks, writing tablets.
I should be growing herbs in a lush garden
　　　overflowing with fragrant sprigs of basil and thyme—
　　　instead I'm at the grocery store
　　　buying pre-washed lettuce in plastic bags,
　　　wilted greens soggy under florescent lights.
I should be smaller, fingernails longer,
　　　scars cleared up, moles gone,
　　　fingers elegant enough to make
　　　spanakopita, dim sum, minced meat pies, samosas.
I should learn cake decorating—
　　　swirling frosting in elaborate creamy peaks
　　　on a cake so magnificent no one ever cuts it.
　　　Instead I'm scarfing down Little Debbie snack cakes
　　　behind a locked office door.

I should be a woman who doesn't say
    I should be,
      no regrets about her growing waistline
      or shrinking life span,
      no regrets about choices made or unmade,
      no efforts at sophistication left.
I should be tired of everything
      unfaithful to everything
      unwilling, unready, unlovely.
I should be, but I'm too familiar
      with what I can't be
      and I can't stop thinking
      I should be that woman
      who can tell one plant from another,
      who saves the early shoots
      of tomatoes and carrots
      instead of mowing them down,
      mistaking them for weeds.

BIOGRAPHICAL NOTE

Allison Joseph lives, writes, and teaches in Carbondale, Illinois, where she directs the MFA Program in Creative Writing at Southern Illinois University. She serves as Editor and Poetry Editor of *Crab Orchard Review*. Her books and chapbooks include *What Keeps Us Here* (Ampersand Press), *Soul Train* (Carnegie Mellon University Press), *In Every Seam* (University of Pittsburgh Press), *Worldly Pleasures* (Word Tech Communications), *Imitation of Life* (Carnegie Mellon UP), *Voice: Poems* (Mayapple Press), *My Father's Kites* (Steel Toe Books), *Trace Particles* (Backbone Press), *Little Epiphanies* (NightBallet Press), *Mercurial* (Mayapple Press), *Mortal Rewards* (White Violet Press), *Multitudes* (Word Poetry), *The Purpose of Hands* (Glass Lyre Press), *Double Identity* (Singing Bone Press), *Corporal Muse* (Sibling Rivalry), and *What Once You Loved* (Barefoot Muse Press). She is the literary partner and wife of poet and editor Jon Tribble.